Who Was Walt Disney?

Who Was
Walt Disney?

by Whitney Stewart

illustrated by Nancy Harrison

Penguin Workshop

To Christoph, a great young artist—WS

PENGUIN WORKSHOP
An Imprint of Penguin Random House LLC, New York

Text copyright © 2009 by Whitney Stewart. Illustrations copyright © 2009 by Nancy Harrison. Cover illustration copyright © 2009 by Penguin Random House LLC. All rights reserved. Published by Penguin Workshop, an imprint of Penguin Random House LLC, New York. PENGUIN and PENGUIN WORKSHOP are trademarks of Penguin Books Ltd. WHO HQ & Design is a registered trademark of Penguin Random House LLC. MICKEY MOUSE and other Disney characters mentioned in this book are registered trademarks of The Walt Disney Company. Printed in the USA.

Visit us online at www.penguinrandomhouse.com.

Library of Congress Control Number: 2008037460

ISBN 9780448450520

45 44 43 42 41 40

Contents

Who Was
Walt Disney?

Walt Disney liked being the class clown.
He once said that he would do anything for
attention. His schoolmates in Marceline,
Missouri, loved his performances.

Once he caught a field mouse and made a
leash for it out of string. He waltzed into class
and paraded his new pet around the room.

Somebody saw the little critter and screamed. Walt's teacher marched right over, put an end to the mischief, and punished Walt. But he didn't care. He and his mouse were famous for a day.

Walt Disney didn't know it then. But one day another mouse—one named Mickey—would make him famous all over the world.

Chapter 1
The Farm

On December 5, 1901, Walter Elias Disney was born in an upstairs bedroom of a two-story cottage on North Tripp Avenue in Chicago. Walt's father, Elias, had built the house himself.

Walt's mother, Flora, was trained as a teacher. But she gave up a career to raise her five children. She was as friendly and warm as her husband was short-tempered and stern.

By the time Walt was four, the neighborhood was growing rough. So the family moved to a farm in Marceline, Missouri. It was the happiest time in Walt's childhood.

Walt loved his new home. Even though Marceline was a small town, it was still exciting

for Walt to head down to Main Street with all its little stores.

Around the farm were weeping willows and apple, peach, and plum trees. Walt watched rabbits, squirrels, opossums, foxes, and raccoons scurry around the pond.

He liked to ride on pigs even though he

often fell off and landed in mud. And he and his friends trotted on Charley, an old farm horse. Charley charged through the trees without caring about his riders. Walt had to jump off to keep from bonking his head on a branch.

Walt's parents and older brothers—Herbert, Raymond, and Roy—were too busy with farm chores to take Walt to school. So he didn't start until he was almost seven. By then, his younger sister Ruth, who was five, was ready for school, too. Walt said that starting school with his younger sister "was the most embarrassing thing that could happen to a fellow."

After school, Walt fished and skinny-dipped. In winter he went sledding or skating on a frozen creek. On Sundays the Disneys visited neighbors. Sometimes Elias played fiddle. It was one of the few times he saw his father having a good time.

Walt always wanted to entertain people, to make them have a good time. Once a group of

actors came to town to perform *Peter Pan*. It was about a boy who never grows up. Walt loved the play and got to play Peter in his school's production of the play. His brother Roy hooked up wires to lift Walt into the air. To the audience it looked like he was flying. But the wires broke. And Walt went flying into the surprised crowd.

Almost as soon as he could hold a pencil, Walt spent hours and hours drawing. He told everybody that he was an artist. His proudest possessions were crayons and drawing paper from his Aunt Margaret.

Walt definitely did have talent. His neighbor Doc Sherwood thought Walt was so good that he asked for a picture of his horse. The horse wouldn't stand still, and Walt had trouble drawing his portrait. But Doc Sherwood and his wife praised the picture. It made Walt very proud.

Even drawing could get Walt into trouble. One day he discovered a barrel of black tar. It was as

soft as paint. He and Ruth dipped big sticks into the tar and drew pictures all over the side of their white house. Their parents were not at all happy when they saw the artwork. The tar wouldn't come off!

Chapter 2
Newspaper Boy

Farm life was fun for Walt but hard for his father. Elias couldn't seem to grow good crops. The family never had enough money. Worrying made his father's temper worse. So Walt avoided him as much as possible. He was much closer to his gentle, smiling mother.

When Elias became sick with typhoid, Flora had no choice but to sell the farm.

Walt was heartbroken about leaving Marceline. He started crying at the sight of a farmer buying the young colt that he and Roy had tamed. The colt whinnied at Walt. He ran after him and hugged him; then the farmer led the colt away.

The Disneys' next move was to Kansas City where Elias ran a newspaper route for the *Kansas*

City Times. Walt had to pitch in, too. He started delivering papers at nine years old. He had to get up every morning before sunrise. Sometimes he was so tired that he curled up in a doorway and fell asleep. When he awoke, he ran to finish his paper route and get to school.

In class Walt had a hard time paying attention.
One teacher called him the "second dumbest" in
her class. He often daydreamed or thought up
ways to make his classmates laugh. He liked to
draw funny characters on the blackboard. Or he'd
draw an animal in the corner of the pages in his
textbook. When he flipped the pages, the animal

appeared to move. These were his first cartoons.

Walt admired Abraham Lincoln. So one day he made a stovepipe hat out of cardboard. He put a fake wart on his cheek so he would look like Lincoln. Then he recited the Gettysburg Address for his class. The teacher loved Walt's act. She asked him to perform it for the other classes. That was fine with Walt. He liked showing off.

Walt's best friend was also named Walt. He liked to perform, too. The two Walts dressed up like the film comedian Charlie Chaplin and his enemy, the Count. They tried out their act in talent contests. One time they won a prize of twenty-five cents each.

CHARLIE CHAPLIN

IN THE EARLY DAYS OF HOLLYWOOD MOVIES, CHARLIE CHAPLIN WAS ONE OF THE MOST FAMOUS ACTORS. HE WAS ALSO A WRITER, DIRECTOR, PRODUCER, AND COMPOSER. HE WAS BORN IN ENGLAND IN 1889 AND STARRED IN OVER EIGHTY FILMS BEFORE HE DIED IN 1977.

CHARLIE CREATED A FUNNY BUT SAD CHARACTER CALLED THE LITTLE TRAMP WHO STARRED IN MANY SILENT MOVIES. THE LITTLE TRAMP WORE A TIGHT COAT, REALLY BAGGY PANTS, BIG SHOES, AND A DERBY HAT. HE CARRIED A BAMBOO CANE AND WALKED WITH HIS TOES TURNED OUT AND WAS VERY POLITE. AND HE ALWAYS GOT HIMSELF INTO RIDICULOUS SITUATIONS.

WALT DISNEY MODELED HIS FIRST MICKEY MOUSE ON CHARLIE CHAPLIN.

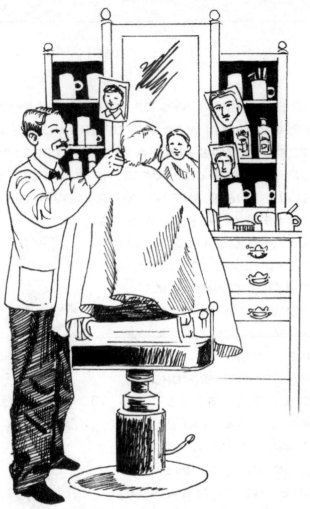

Walt's artistic talent earned him free haircuts from the local barber. Neighbors started going to the barbershop just to see Walt's newest pictures on the wall. Walt loved his little bit of fame.

At fifteen, Walt got to see more of the country. He had a summer job working on a train that traveled between Kansas City, Missouri, and Spiro, Oklahoma. He walked up the aisle selling newspapers, candy, and soda, and chatting with people. Sometimes the engineer let him ride in the coal car. For Walt that was heaven. All his life, he loved trains. They carried you to new places, new adventures.

Chapter 3
Seeing the World

In 1917 once again the Disneys had to move. The newspaper route wasn't bringing in enough money. So Elias decided the family should return to Chicago. There he invested in a fruit juice and jelly company. Maybe this time his luck would change.

In Chicago, Walt attended McKinley High School. Once again he was bored in all of his classes. The only thing he liked was drawing cartoons for the school newspaper. After a year he dropped out of school.

Even though he wasn't sure what he wanted to be, Walt had faith in himself. He was sure that one day he would be a big success—maybe as a newspaper cartoonist or maybe doing

something in show
business.

At night he took
art classes at the
Chicago Academy
of Fine Arts. He
also bought himself
a movie camera. He
and a new friend,
Russell Maas, made
short films together.
They worked out

a comedy act, but it must have been pretty bad.
When the boys tried out their act at a theater,
they got kicked off the stage.

To support himself, Walt applied for a job
with the post office. The boss said he was too
young, so Walt went home, changed his clothes,
put on a man's hat, and drew a mustache on his
face. Then he went back to the post office, talked

to the same man again and this time he got the job!

While Walt was working at the post office, two of his brothers—Herbert and Roy—were serving in the army. It was wartime. World War I. The United States had joined the fight against Germany and was sending thousands of American troops over to Europe.

Walt felt as if he was missing out on all the action. To him the war seemed like an adventure. But he was too young to enlist. Finally he convinced his mother to sign papers to permit him to drive an ambulance. He set sail for France in November of 1918. He had not yet turned seventeen, but he was about to see a whole new world.

The thing was Walt never got near a battlefield. To his disappointment, the fighting had already ended by the time Walt reached France. Instead of rescuing wounded soldiers, he spent much of his time driving officers around, running errands, and drawing. He drew cartoons all over the canvas flaps of the ambulance.

Walt made extra cash in a dishonest way. He and a friend found some helmets of German soldiers. They scuffed them up and shot holes in them. Then Walt's friend sold them as real war souvenirs.

Walt returned home a year later in October 1919. He was almost eighteen. His family hardly recognized him because he had grown so much taller. He had filled out and looked like a man. Walt was also hooked on cigarettes—a terrible habit he never quit.

Elias Disney wanted his son to work in Chicago at the jelly factory. But Walt wasn't interested.

Against his father's wishes, he decided to go

23

back to Kansas City and find work as an artist.

Walt Disney was ready to strike out on his own.

Chapter 4
Drawings that Move

In Kansas City, Walt teamed up with another artist. He had a very unusual name . . . Ub

UB IWERKS

Iwerks. Ub was shy and serious. Not at all like Walt. Ub was also very talented. The two started their own company. They hoped to create art for ads and signs. They had plenty of ideas. They were missing only one thing— customers. The shop closed after only a month.

Soon after, Walt and Ub found jobs at the Kansas City Slide Company. It turned out to be a lucky break. The slide company changed Walt's life. He learned all about animation.

Animation is a film of drawings that move. Cartoons. In 1920 cartoons were something new. Audiences were amazed to watch drawings of funny people and animals actually moving on the screen.

ANIMATION BASICS

AN ARTIST CREATES SIMPLE ANIMATION
(FOR EXAMPLE, A DOG WAGGING ITS TAIL) BY
DRAWING THE SAME CHARACTER OVER AND OVER
ON SEPARATE PIECES OF PAPER. IN EACH
DRAWING, THE POSITION OF THE TAIL WILL BE A
LITTLE DIFFERENT. WHEN THE PIECES OF PAPER
ARE FLIPPED REALLY FAST, TO THE HUMAN EYE
THE TAIL APPEARS TO BE MOVING. FOR FILMS,
PROFESSIONAL ANIMATORS CREATE THE ILLUSION
OF MOTION BY RECORDING THE SCENE CHANGES
FRAME BY FRAME.

Artists competed with each other to invent new techniques for cartoons. Walt wanted to get in on the action. So he went to the library and took out a book called *Animated Cartoons: How They Are Made, Their Origin and Development,* by Edwin G. Lutz. He studied the book. Then he set up a studio in the shed behind his house.

Every evening he drew cartoon characters in different positions and filmed them. It might take eighteen drawings just to show a person raising an arm. Animation takes lots of time. But hard work never stopped Walt.

He called his cartoons *Laugh-O-Grams.* They were silent, full of slapstick humor, and only lasted a couple of minutes. Some were based on fairy tales. But Walt would change the story a little to make it funnier. After selling a *Laugh-O-Gram* cartoon to the Newman theaters in Kansas City, he started up a small company to make more.

Walt recruited artists to help him make cartoons. After all, he couldn't do all the drawing himself. The problem was he couldn't afford to pay a steady salary. Instead, he promised to share any money earned from the cartoons. His friend

Ub Iwerks and a few other young men joined Walt in his new business. They spent the day drawing characters, making up jokes, and goofing around with a movie camera.

Walt worked on one film called *Alice's Wonderland*. It was about a real little girl named Alice, played by a four-year-old actress named Virginia Davis. Walt's Alice finds herself in a cartoon world. Mixing live actors with animation was something new. But before he finished *Alice's Wonderland*, Walt's company went bankrupt. He even had to sell his movie camera.

Kansas City was not the center of the entertainment business. Walt knew that. If he wanted to make it big, he had better go where movies were made.

Hollywood.

MAKING AN ANIMATED DISNEY FILM

WALT DISNEY AND HIS WRITERS STARTED PLOTTING OUT A STORY SCENE BY SCENE. THEN ANIMATORS DREW EACH CHARACTER IN THOUSANDS OF DIFFERENT POSES TO CREATE THE ACTION. INKERS TRACED THE LINES OF EACH DRAWING ON PIECES OF CLEAR CELLULOID. PAINTERS COLORED ON THE CELLULOID DRAWINGS. OTHER ARTISTS PAINTED BACKGROUND SCENES. AFTER CAMERA OPERATORS PHOTOGRAPHED EACH DRAWING ON THE RIGHT BACKGROUND, SOUND SPECIALISTS RECORDED THE VOICES AND SOUND EFFECTS AND ADDED IN THE BACKGROUND MUSIC. ONCE EVERYTHING WAS DONE THERE WAS STILL ONE MORE THING NEEDED—WALT HAD TO GIVE HIS FINAL APPROVAL.

Chapter 5
Hollywood

After World War I, Hollywood became home to film studios such as Universal, Paramount, Warner Brothers, and Metro-Goldwyn-Mayer (MGM). Movies were now a big business.

In August 1923, Walt packed a cardboard suitcase with his clothes and drawing materials. He bought a train ticket to California where his

older brother Roy was already living. Walt moved in with an uncle, paying a few dollars a month for room and board.

Walt had big dreams for himself. But he certainly didn't look like much of a success. He was stick-thin and wore shabby clothing. He spiffed himself up as best he could and went to every movie studio in town. Nobody offered him a job. So, he went back to his old idea of making and selling cartoons.

In October, he finally got a break. A woman named Margaret Winkler saw and liked what Walt had done in *Alice's Wonderland*. She agreed to pay Walt for a series of Alice cartoons, which she would sell to theaters.

This was terrific news except for one thing. Walt had only three months to make a new film. His young actress, Virginia Davis, still lived in Kansas City. Also, Walt needed money to make the movie. He didn't even have a movie camera much less a studio or artists to work with him.

Walt turned to his brother Roy for help. Roy was eight years older than Walt. Unlike Walt, Roy was practical. He had a good head for business. So the two formed the Disney Brothers Studio.

With a loan from their uncle and some money from their parents, Walt and Roy set up shop in a small office on Kingswell Avenue. Walt bought himself a movie camera, and he persuaded Virginia Davis and her family to move to Hollywood.

At first, Walt did all the creative work in the

ROY AND WALT DISNEY

studio. He thought up the story for each of the Alice movies. He directed his child star. He drew all the cartoon characters and put the live action and animation together. He worked so hard that his first film was finished ahead of schedule.

But making a whole series of Alice films was too much work for one man. So Walt hired three men to operate the cameras and help with the animation. He also hired three women to ink and paint the black-and-white cartoon drawings. One of the young women was small and pretty with

LILLIAN BOUNDS

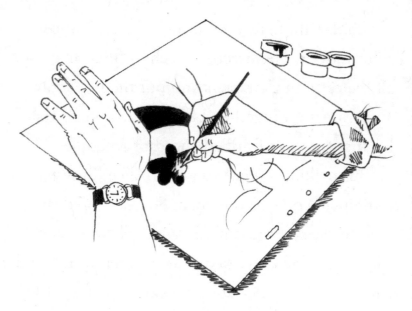

dark hair. She was named Lillian Bounds.

Walt also worried that his own drawings were not good enough. He wanted his cartoon films to be the best in the business. So he got in touch with Ub Iwerks. Walt convinced Ub to move out to California and join the Disney studio.

Ub was talented and fast. He could produce great drawings in no time. Over the years Ub did more and more of the drawing while Walt focused on thinking up the stories and directing.

Together they created a new character named Oswald the Lucky Rabbit and started making a series of Oswald cartoons. It was a smart decision. Oswald was a hit.

The studio began selling cartoons on a regular basis. Business was so good, in fact, that Walt and Roy moved to bigger offices on Hyperion Avenue. And Walt changed the name of the company. Instead of Disney Brothers Studio, he wanted to call it Walt Disney Studios.

Did Roy mind? It seems that he didn't. All Roy said was, "If that's the way you want it," it was okay with him. After all Walt was the one making the cartoons.

Walt was under a lot of pressure now. He had to make lots of Oswald cartoons and do it quickly. He became short-tempered and irritable. He took his worries out on his employees. Some quit because they couldn't stand his insulting remarks. "Walt could make you feel real bad when he wanted to," one of them said.

Then something really nasty happened. Something Walt never expected and didn't deserve. A man named Charlie Mintz whose company was buying Oswald the Lucky Rabbit cartoons hired away most of Walt's artists. Mintz decided he didn't need Walt anymore. With Walt's own artists, he could make and sell Oswald cartoons without Walt Disney Studios.

What Charlie Mintz did wasn't actually against the law, but it was still wrong.

Walt was so upset that he couldn't eat or sleep. Not only had he lost Oswald but he had been double-crossed. The only way he could save his business was to create another cartoon character, an even better one than Oswald.

Walt worked like mad on a new idea and kept it secret. Only a few people—Ub who did the drawing; Roy, who was always loyal to his brother; and Lillian who inked the drawings— knew about the new character.

The new character was going to be a mouse.

Chapter 6
A Mouse Named Mickey

Lillian Bounds was from Idaho. She had moved to Hollywood in 1923. She was twenty-six years old. Her boss, Walt, liked her spunky nature. Her short bobbed hair bounced when she laughed.

Often Walt would give Lillian a ride home after work. He was very proud of the new car he'd bought—a Ford roadster. The two got to know

each other on those rides. Finally Walt asked Lillian out on a date. He even said he'd buy himself a new suit for the occasion. Lillian agreed, and Walt went shopping. Confident as he often seemed, he was shy around girls. In fact, he was twenty-two and still hadn't had a serious girlfriend.

Walt showed up at Lillian's door dressed in a gray-green, double-breasted suit holding theater tickets. Lillian was charmed, and off they went.

On July 13, 1925, Walt and Lillian were married. They spent their honeymoon at Mount Rainier. On their wedding night, Walt had such a bad toothache that he couldn't sleep. To take his mind off the pain, he left their room and helped a porter shine shoes all night.

The next morning he went to a dentist and had his tooth pulled. It certainly wasn't the most fun way to start off a marriage. But Walt had a good story to tell.

Lillian quit her job at the studio but staying home was lonely. Walt spent such long hours at work. (In later years, sometimes after dinner Lillian would go back to the studio with Walt and go to sleep on a sofa while he kept on working.)

For Christmas Walt decided to find company for Lillian. He wrapped a big hatbox with a ribbon and presented it to her on Christmas morning. Expecting a hat, Lillian opened the box

and out popped a furry orange puppy. She named it Sunnee. Soon Sunnee went everywhere with her. As for Walt, he was just as crazy about Sunnee as Lillian was.

Every night Walt would tell Lillian how his new cartoon character was coming along. One story is that the mouse was first named Mortimer. But Lillian didn't like the name. Mortimer sounded too fancy. Instead she suggested Mickey.

No one can be sure if this story is exactly true. Walt often stretched the truth to make a story more interesting. But one way or another, the new cartoon character got the name Mickey Mouse. He was skinny with stick legs, a long tail, and a sharp face. He didn't look that much like the Mickey Mouse everyone knows today. He also wasn't as nice. Early cartoons starring Mickey Mouse often show him playing mean tricks on other characters. (As Mickey became everybody's hero, Disney saw he needed another character that was naughty, greedy, and rude in a funny way. That character was Donald Duck.)

Like most movies and cartoons at that time,

the first Mickey Mouse cartoon, called *Plane Crazy*, was silent and in black and white. In *Plane Crazy*, Mickey was a daredevil pilot who tries to impress his girlfriend Minnie. The cartoon character came out not long after Charles Lindbergh became the first person to fly across the Atlantic Ocean.

CHARLES LINDBERGH

Mickey Mouse is so hugely popular today that it is hard to believe that Walt had no luck selling his first two Mickey cartoons. But it's true. No theater wanted to show Walt's mouse cartoons.

Never one to give up, Walt asked himself what would make Mickey more exciting. His answer was . . . sound. The first movie with sound came out in 1927. It was called *The Jazz Singer* and starred a popular actor named Al Jolson. But as of yet, there had never been a cartoon with sound. If Walt could do that, it would certainly grab the attention of audiences.

In *Steamboat Willie*, Mickey Mouse whistles. His girlfriend Minnie says, "yoo-hoo." There was also music and other sound effects like doors slamming.

Steamboat Willie was by far the best sound cartoon of its time. The manager of the Colony Theater in New York City agreed to show it. And audiences loved it. Soon other theaters started showing it. Walt quickly added soundtracks to his two earlier Mickey cartoons and now was able to sell them to theaters as well. (For later cartoons, Walt recorded himself doing the voices of both Mickey and Minnie.)

Now something really surprising happened. A manager of a theater in Ocean Park, California, came up with a great gimmick. He invited kids to come to his theater and watch hours and hours of Mickey Mouse cartoons. All the kids who showed up became members of a club called the Mickey Mouse Club. There were pie-eating contests and marble tournaments for club members.

Walt visited the theater one afternoon and watched one thousand Mickey Mouse Club members screaming for their cartoon hero. Walt decided to start more clubs in other cities.

Mickey Mouse Clubs started to spring up all over America. At their meetings, kids recited the Mickey Mouse Club pledge: "Mickey Mice do not swear, smoke, cheat, or lie." There was also a special club song.

The Mickey Mouse Clubs made Mickey Mouse cartoons even more popular. And the cartoons made even more kids want to join a Mickey Mouse Club.

Soon a Mickey Mouse cartoon strip, drawn

by Ub Iwerks, was appearing in forty newspapers around the country. Kids went crazy buying Mickey Mouse dolls, buttons, pencils, toothbrushes, and books.

Walt had done something new, something big, just as he always hoped he would.

And it was just the beginning.

Chapter 7
Ups and Downs

Walt Disney was on top of the world when trouble hit the studio again. A dishonest distributor wanted control of Mickey Mouse. Walt had lost Oswald. He was not going to let Mickey get away. Roy worked out a deal so that the Disneys kept ownership of Mickey. The distributor, however, did manage to hire away Ub Iwerks.

Why did Ub Iwerks leave?

Ub said that Walt always was complaining about the work Ub did. And Walt liked to take all the credit for Disney cartoons. According to Ub, Walt couldn't even draw a proper Mickey Mouse. One time a boy begged

Walt for a drawing of Mickey with Walt's autograph. Walt asked Ub to draw it, and then Walt would sign it. Ub got so mad that he told Walt to draw it himself and stomped off.

Losing Ub was hard. Walt was angry and hurt. But he hired new animators to join his team. They quickly realized that Walt was the most important man in the studio even if he didn't do the drawing. He chose what cartoons to make. He worked on the story development and artwork. He made all the final decisions. If the new animators didn't like it, they had to keep quiet or quit.

In the early 1930s, Walt Disney Studios produced many short cartoons called *Silly Symphonies*. As always Walt wanted to do something new. *Three Little Pigs* had much more of a plot. The story of the pigs and the hungry wolf came from *The Green Fairy Book*, by Andrew Lang. It was Walt's idea to put in a song. It was called "Who's Afraid of the Big Bad Wolf?" People came

out of theaters whistling the peppy tune. The song
seemed to cheer people up.

Three Little Pigs came out in 1933. Many
people needed cheering up. It was a time called
the Great Depression. Thousands of companies
had gone out of business. Millions of workers
lost their jobs. People lost their homes. Fewer

THE GREAT DEPRESSION

IN THE 1920S, MANY AMERICANS BOUGHT AND SOLD STOCKS (SHARES OF COMPANIES). SOME PEOPLE BECAME RICH FROM TRADING ON THE STOCK MARKET. BUT IN 1929, MANY OF THESE STOCKS BECAME WORTHLESS, AND THE STOCK MARKET CRASHED.

BANKS CLOSED. MILLIONS OF PEOPLE LOST THEIR
JOBS. BECAUSE OF UNEMPLOYMENT, PEOPLE HAD
LITTLE MONEY FOR HOMES, CARS, OR FOOD. THEY'D
STAND FOR HOURS IN LINE TO RECEIVE BASICS, LIKE
A LOAF OF BREAD. THE GREAT DEPRESSION ENDED
IN THE EARLY 1940S.

families had money to spend on extras like going to movie theaters.

But Walt Disney Studios was doing fine. By 1930 a company called Technicolor was producing good color film for movies. Walt is

said to have shouted, "At last! We can show a rainbow on the screen." Walt's *Flowers and Trees*, about two trees who fall in love, was the first cartoon in full color. It won an Academy Award.

Everyone at Disney worked long hours. But nobody worked harder than Walt. He drove himself to the point of collapse. He was exhausted and more moody than ever.

He was also upset because he and Lillian were having trouble having children. Walt worried that he might never be a father. He couldn't sleep at night. He often cried. He became so sick that his doctor insisted he take a long vacation to recover from stress.

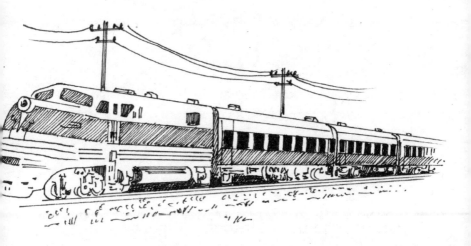

In the fall of 1931, Walt and Lillian took a train all across the country to Washington, D.C. Being on a train was always relaxing and fun for

Walt. They took a boat trip through the Panama Canal. He and Lillian lounged on deck chairs and had romantic dinners. When the Disneys

returned home, Walt took up sports to ease stress—ice-skating, swimming, horseback riding, and polo.

In 1933, Lillian became pregnant. Walt was thrilled. He wrote his family about all of the

pink and blue baby items in the nursery. On
December 18, a healthy baby girl was born—
Diane Marie Disney.

Lillian could not have any more children after
Diane. So in 1937 the Disneys adopted a baby
girl and named her Sharon Mae.

Walt did everything he could to give his

daughters a happy home life. And he always had a
movie camera in his hand to record family fun. He

read to his girls, took them on outings, acted out stories for them, and took them bike riding at the

studio. He even built a giant playhouse for them that looked like it was made for Snow White.

As for fancy Hollywood parties, Walt had no interest in them. He liked staying home, eating

chili and beans on crackers. Roy and his wife and son lived nearby. The two families saw a lot of each other.

Walt's parents, however, were still living far away in Portland, Oregon. So Walt and Roy

decided to buy a house in California for them. The Disneys could all get together for backyard barbecues.

The house was a wonderful gift, meant to bring joy. Instead, it brought terrible sorrow. There was something wrong with the heating system. Suddenly, one day in 1938, Elias and Flora became sick from breathing in poisonous gas that was leaking. Elias recovered but, sadly, Flora died.

Walt was so upset that for the rest of his life he refused to talk about his mother's death.

Chapter 8
Snow White

Walt Disney was always looking for the next big idea. He was always pushing the boundaries of what could be done in a cartoon. He and his artists perfected sound and color. Walt didn't stop there.

In 1933 he decided to make a full-length animated film. Up until then, cartoons were short. They lasted only a few minutes. In theaters they were shown before a full-length movie. Yet Walt knew that kids would sit watching hours of different Mickey Mouse cartoons. So why wouldn't they sit through one long animated movie if it was good enough?

Besides being short, cartoons were always full of slapstick gags. A full-length animated movie, however, needed more than humor. Walt had to have a story with romance and drama and excitement. The famous fairy tale, *Snow*

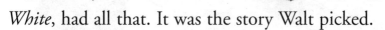

White, had all that. It was the story Walt picked.

It took years to create *Snow White and the Seven Dwarfs*. More than a quarter of a million drawings were done for the eighty-three minute movie. Walt was in charge of every step of production.

At meetings he acted out scenes for his animation team. The artists copied Walt's expressions and movements into their drawings.

He wanted each character to seem as real as a live actor. Yes, there would be funny scenes. But there would also be parts where people would cry or hold their breath in fear.

The backgrounds were important, too. They could not look flat and two-dimensional. For example, the house of the seven dwarfs had to look as if it were solid and in real space. A special multi-plane camera also helped make everything look three-dimensional.

Disney artists spent more than three years making *Snow White*. One spent almost a year drawing a funny scene of the dwarfs eating soup.

And it didn't even end up in the movie!

Roy had one of the hardest jobs. He had to come up with the money to make *Snow White*. The studio borrowed more than one and a half million dollars. This was an incredible sum of money for a cartoon. And what if the film flopped? How would the studio pay it back?

Snow White and the Seven Dwarfs opened

CARTHAY CIRCLE THEATRE

on December 21, 1937, at the Carthay Circle
Theatre in Los Angeles.

Famous Hollywood stars came dressed in
evening gowns and tuxedos.

The audience gasped at the beauty of the

film. At the end the applause was like thunder.

Time magazine put Walt on the cover and called *Snow White* a masterpiece. Walt won a special Academy Award. (It had a golden Oscar surrounded by seven smaller Oscars.)

Over the next few years, Disney produced three more wonderful movies in animation: *Fantasia*, *Pinocchio*, and *Bambi*. However, none matched the film magic of *Snow White*. To this day it remains one of the most popular movies ever made.

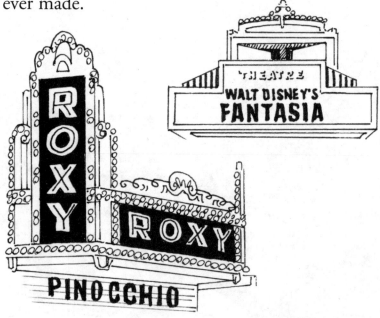

Chapter 9
The Strike

Snow White made so much money that Roy and Walt bought fifty-one acres of land for a new studio in Burbank, California.

In 1940 everyone moved into the complex. The company was now a big business. There were hundreds of employees. The animators worked in one building. And inkers, painters, and special effects artists worked in others. Walt thought that his employees would be happy to leave their old cramped spaces and work in modern, air-conditioned buildings. But he was wrong.

In the old days, all the Disney employees worked closely together and felt like family. Now they were separated from each other. People rarely saw Walt. There were complaints that the studio felt like a big factory.

On top of that, once again the studio was having money trouble.

A lot of money came from selling Disney cartoons to theaters in countries all over Europe. But since 1939, war—World War II—had been raging in Europe. The market for Disney's films there dried up. So Roy had to cut wages, and this made employees angry. They said they would stop working if Walt and Roy didn't listen to their complaints. Walt held a meeting and tried to calm people down. It didn't work.

On May 29, 1941, hundreds of Disney workers went on strike. That meant they refused to work until their demands were met. They stood outside the studio entrance, shouting at anyone who dared go to work. When Walt drove up each morning, workers screamed and banged on his car.

The strike lasted nine weeks. It upset Walt terribly. He believed that the Disney studio had always been fair to employees. He felt betrayed. His health suffered again from all the stress. In early August, he went to South America. While he was away Roy settled with the strike leaders. The employees got their pay demands.

But the strike changed Walt. He refused to see that any of the workers had honest complaints. He was very bitter. Then in September his father Elias died. Now both Walt's parents were gone. And his next full-length cartoon, *Dumbo,* about a flying elephant, was not the success Walt was hoping for. It came out in October of 1941.

Everything changed at the studio after December 7, 1941. That was when the Japanese army bombed an American naval base at Pearl Harbor, Hawaii. Now the United States was in the war, too. American soldiers were fighting on two fronts—in the Pacific and in Europe.

The U.S. Army took over Walt's studio. Training films for soldiers were needed. Walt

PEARL HARBOR

ON SUNDAY, DECEMBER 7, 1941, THE JAPANESE BOMBED A NAVAL BASE AT PEARL HARBOR IN HAWAII. THE SURPRISE ATTACK DESTROYED U.S. WARSHIPS AND PLANES AND KILLED TWENTY-FOUR HUNDRED PEOPLE. AMERICANS WERE SHOCKED BY THE NEWS. PRESIDENT FRANKLIN ROOSEVELT DECLARED WAR ON JAPAN THE NEXT DAY. THREE DAYS LATER, OUR COUNTRY DECLARED WAR ON GERMANY AND ITALY. WORLD WAR II

FRANKLIN D. ROOSEVELT

ENDED IN EUROPE IN MAY 1945. JAPAN DID NOT SURRENDER UNTIL AUGUST 1945 AFTER THE UNITED STATES DROPPED AN ATOMIC BOMB ON THE CITIES OF HIROSHIMA AND NAGASAKI, JAPAN.

had a hard time feeling creative doing this kind of work.

Walt used Donald Duck in several cartoons for the U.S. Army. In one, Donald plays a skinny American soldier who becomes a hero. In another film, Donald Duck is living a miserable life in

Nazi Germany. At the end, it turns out to be a bad dream. Donald wakes up, safe and happy in the United States. This kind of film was to make Americans feel proud of their country.

The war ended in 1945. Walt could now go back to making his own movies. Several live-action adventure movies came out. But audiences didn't like *Treasure Island, Swiss Family Robinson,* or *20,000 Leagues Under the Sea* as much as they had liked *Snow White*. One Disney movie, *Song of the South*, made many people angry. The main character is an old African American man named Uncle Remus who lives on a southern plantation. The NAACP, an early civil rights organization,

felt the movie made the lives of slaves seem happy
(even though the film was set after the Civil War
had ended). Black Americans were very upset.
Critics said Walt Disney was out of touch.

Walt turned to making nature movies like
Seal Island, stories that filmed real animals but
had a made-up story. Walt did not pour his heart
into these films the way he had with his classics.
Maybe making movies was starting to bore him a
little.

Or maybe it was because Walt was already
thinking about the next big thing.

Chapter 10
A Fantasy World

In some ways Walt Disney always remained a kid at heart. When he took his daughters to the merry-go-round in Griffith Park, he'd get on a horse and ride, too.

At home Walt spent hours tinkering with wind-up toys and model trains. He even had a real little railroad built in his big backyard. On weekends, Walt put on an engineer's cap. He'd take his daughters and friends for a ride. Afterward he'd

whip up goopy banana splits that nobody could finish. It was good, wholesome fun.

That started Walt thinking. What if there were a place where families, not just kids, could go and have fun together. It would be like an amusement park, only cleaner, different, better. It would have a village like Marceline, Missouri. Stores would sell Disney clothes and toys. There'd be a little railroad, a movie theater, and rides. Lots of rides.

Roy wasn't wild about the Disneyland idea. Who will pay for it, he asked? But Walt already had the answer.

Television had always fascinated Walt. He saw that it was the next big thing. All through the 1920s and 1930s people tuned into popular radio shows. But you could only listen to the radio—you couldn't see anything.

Television brought about the end of radio shows. Many filmmakers also thought of TV as the enemy. The little screen was taking away the audience for big-screen pictures. Not Walt. He saw TV as another way to entertain people. He thought that in return for a Disney TV show, a network would invest in his theme park.

Walt was right.

ABC started running a show that featured Disney cartoons and some live-action skits. It was a big hit. The only show that was more popular was *I Love Lucy*, starring the comedian Lucille Ball.

Walt was the host of the show. He talked to viewers in a friendly, grandfatherly way. Before long, kids all knew Walt Disney's face. He was a star.

The Mickey Mouse Club was another hit for ABC. In every episode there was always a newsreel, a cartoon, and songs and dances performed by a group of young actors called Mouseketeers. The

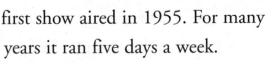

first show aired in 1955. For many years it ran five days a week.

He also created a western miniseries called *Davy Crockett*. Davy Crockett was a real-life frontiersman from Tennessee who lived in the early 1800s. To play Davy, Walt chose a good-looking young actor named Fess Parker. There were only three episodes of *Davy Crockett*. But every kid wanted a coonskin cap like Davy's. Every kid

DAVY CROCKETT

knew the words to the theme song.

The studio made a lot of money in television. Television helped Walt build his Disneyland dream. As with all of the other big Disney projects, Walt was in control. He loved working on the theme park. If he wanted to create a jungle, he did. If a lake wasn't big enough, he had it made bigger.

Disneyland opened on July 17, 1955, in Anaheim, California. Just four days earlier he and Lillian had their thirtieth wedding anniversary.

Opening day did not go smoothly. Crowds stood in line in one hundred degree heat. Some of the rides weren't working. The train didn't lead anywhere—it came to a dead end. There were not enough trash cans or water fountains.

But Walt had things fixed right away. Soon the place was spotless. Everyone who worked there was polite and cheerful. (They had to go to "Disney University" to learn exactly how to behave toward visitors.)

People all over the world were flocking to Disneyland. They could spend time in Fantasyland with its fairy-tale castle and fairy-tale characters in costume. They could look for hippos and other wild animals in Adventureland, or ride on the Mark Twain Riverboat. There was Main Street that looked very much like the one in Marceline, Missouri.

Walt enjoyed Disneyland as much as anyone. But he had to disguise himself in a floppy hat and sunglasses or else fans would mob him. Sometimes a child still recognized him. Walt would put his finger to his lips and secretly slip the child an autograph.

After hours, Walt had Disneyland all to himself. He drove a mini fire engine through the streets or relaxed in his private apartment over the firehouse on Main Street. Already he was thinking about the next big thing—a city of the future. Walt's plan for EPCOT—Experimental Prototype Community of Tomorrow—included monorails and underground roads to keep children safe from cars. City streets would be designed to look like different places from around the world. It would be just the kind of place Walt would want to live in himself!

EPCOT

EPCOT IS A THEME PARK AT WALT DISNEY WORLD IN ORLANDO, FLORIDA. THE WORD EPCOT STANDS FOR EXPERIMENTAL PROTOTYPE COMMUNITY OF TOMORROW. IN THE 1960S, WALT DISNEY PLANNED EPCOT TO BE A MODEL TOWN WHERE PEOPLE LIVED AND WORKED. THERE WOULD BE NO CRIME, SLUMS, OR TRAFFIC. AFTER HIS DEATH, THE DISNEY COMPANY DECIDED THAT IT

DID NOT WANT TO RUN A CITY, SO THE IDEA FOR EPCOT—WHICH OPENED IN 1982— CHANGED. IT IS A SHOW-CASE FOR DIFFERENT CULTURES AND CUSTOMS OF COUNTRIES ALL AROUND THE WORLD.

Chapter 11
Final Act

Some men slow down as they age, but not Walt Disney. He had too many ideas to quit working.

In 1964 a giant world's fair was held outside of New York City. Some of the best exhibits were

UNISPHERE

designed by Walt Disney. One was called "Great Moments with Mr. Lincoln." An Abraham Lincoln robot got up from a chair. He looked left and right at his audience. Then he shifted his weight from one foot to another and recited a speech about liberty. The robot looked so real that people thought it was an actor.

Walt didn't spend much time at the studios anymore. Making movies didn't interest him. Diane and Sharon were both married. Walt and Lillian became regular babysitters for their grand-children. Walt loved having a house full of little children again.

He often sat on his lawn and watched his wild bunch pile up patio furniture to make backyard

forts and rocket ships. He let the kids spend the
night at Disneyland and explore it when nobody
else was around. And he put some of them into
Disney films, just for fun.

In July 1966, Walt and Lillian celebrated
their forty-first anniversary. They took the whole

family on a cruise to British Columbia. Walt wasn't feeling well. But he enjoyed being with his grandchildren. He let them crawl all over him. When he got tired, he climbed to the upper deck to think. He'd think about EPCOT.

After the trip, Walt didn't get better. Medical tests discovered something very serious. Walt had lung cancer. Walt had smoked cigarettes since his days in France. Until 1964, however, people did not know that smoking caused cancer.

While Walt was in the hospital, Roy came for a visit. He found Walt staring at the ceiling. Walt pointed out where everything was going to go at EPCOT. The next day, December 15, 1966, he

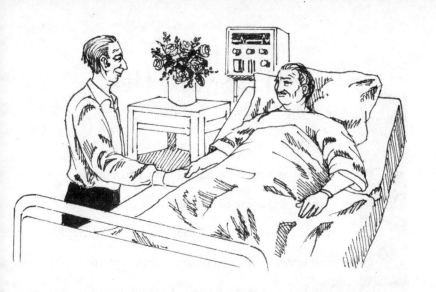

died. Walt Disney was sixty-five years old.

He did not live to see the opening of Walt Disney World in Florida in 1971. But Roy was there. He waited to retire until Walt Disney World was completed.

Walt Disney has been gone for a long time. However, he is still entertaining people through Disney books, records, movies, toys, and his parks all over the world, where each year millions of families come with one idea—to have fun.

TIMELINE OF
WALT DISNEY'S LIFE

1901	Walt is born December 5 in Chicago, Illinois
1906	The Disneys move to a farm in Marceline, Missouri
1910	The Disneys move to Kansas City, Missouri
1917	The Disneys move to Chicago
1918	Walt drives ambulances in France during World War I
1919	Walt opens his first commercial art company
1920	Walt learns animation at the Kansas City Slide Company
1922	Walt makes *Laugh-O-Gram* cartoons
1923	Walt and brother Roy start the Disney Brothers Studio
1925	Marries Lillian Bounds on July 13
1928	Releases Mickey Mouse film called *Steamboat Willie*
1937	Releases *Snow White and the Seven Dwarfs*
1950	Walt appears on TV in *One Hour in Wonderland*
1955	Walt opens Disneyland on July 17
1964	Disney exhibits at the New York World's Fair
1965	Buys lands in Florida for EPCOT
1966	Walt dies of lung cancer on December 15

TIMELINE OF
THE WORLD

Marconi sends his first transatlantic radio signal	1901
Wright Brothers' first flight	1903
Titanic sinks and 1,513 people die	1912
Russian Revolution begins	1917
World War I ends	1918
New York Yankees sign Babe Ruth	1920
Abraham Lincoln Memorial is dedicated	1922
Adolf Hitler publishes his book *Mein Kampf*	1925
Amelia Earhart flies solo across the Atlantic	1932
Dr. Seuss's first children's book is published	1937
Germany invades Poland and World War II begins	1939
Japanese bomb Pearl Harbor and U.S. joins war	1941
World War II ends	1945
Albert Einstein dies	1955
Martin Luther King Jr. gives "I Have a Dream" speech	1963
Beatles' song "Yesterday" becomes a number-one hit in the U.S.	1965
Pampers disposable diapers become popular	1966
Harry Potter and the Sorcerer's Stone published	1998

BIBLIOGRAPHY

Barrier, Michael. **The Animated Man: A Life of Walt Disney.** University of California Press, California, 2007.

*Feinstein, Stephen. **Read About Walt Disney.** Enslow, New Jersey, 2005.

Finch, Christopher. **The Art of Walt Disney: From Mickey Mouse to the Magic Kingdoms.** Harry N. Abrams, Inc., New York, 1975.

Gabler, Neal. **Walt Disney: The Triumph of the American Imagination.** Vintage, New York, 2006.

*Hammontree, Marie. **Walt Disney: Young Movie Maker.** Aladdin, New York, 1997.

Jackson, Kathy Merlock (editor). **Walt Disney: Conversations.** University Press of Mississippi, Mississippi, 2006.

Merritt, Russell and J. B. Kaufman. **Walt in Wonderland: The Silent Films of Walt Disney.** Le Giornate del Cinema Muto, Italy, 1993.

*Preszler, June. **Walt Disney.** Capstone Press, Minnesota, 2003.

*Selden, Bernice. **The Story of Walt Disney: Maker of Magical Worlds.** Yearling, New York, 1989.

*Books for young readers

Here is a list of some of the famous movies made by Walt Disney.

Snow White and the Seven Dwarfs..................1937

Pinocchio..................1940

Fantasia..................1940

Dumbo..................1941

Bambi..................1942

Song of the South..................1946

Cinderella..................1950

Treasure Island..................1950

Alice in Wonderland..................1951

Peter Pan..................1953

20,000 Leagues Under the Sea..................1954

Lady and the Tramp..................1955

Old Yeller..................1957

Sleeping Beauty..................1959

Swiss Family Robinson..................1960

The Parent Trap..................1961

The Sword in the Stone..................1963

Mary Poppins..................1964